Enabling Love

A
Tribute
To
William Meredith

By Tom Kirlin

Winner of the 2019 William Meredith Award in Poetry

A Major Work

Poems are hard to read
Pictures are hard to see
Music is hard to hear
And people are hard to love

But whether from brute need
Or divine energy
At last mind eye and ear
And the great sloth heart will move.

–William Meredith

Enabling Love

A
Tribute
To
William Meredith

By Tom Kirlin

Poets' Choice Publishing

Poets-Choice.com

337 Kitemaug Road
Uncasville, Ct. 06382
MarathonFilm@gmail.com

llustrations © by Stoimen Stoilov
Author's photo by Kate C. Kirlin

Copyright © 2019 Poets' Choice Publishing
All Rights Reserved
Published in the United States of America

Library of Congress Cataloging-in-Publication Pending

ISBN: 978-1-7335400-0-1

Table of Contents

Foreword		7
I.	You Move Among Us	9
II.	The Literate Imagination	19
III.	It Was May	29
IV.	The End of Deception	41
V.	Self-Reckoning	51
VI.	The Center Cannot Hold	65
VII.	Efforts at Speech	73
VIII.	Impartial Laughter	83
Epilogue		89
Examples of Created Systems		93
Artist's Biography		97
Author's Biography		99

Acknowledgements

William Meredith, *Partial Accounts: New and Selected Poems*, Alfred A. Knopf (New York, 1987)

"Why the Soul Loves Catfish," Tom Kirlin, *Under the Potato Moon*, Little Red Tree Publishing, LLC (New London, 2013)

Foreword

This award recognizes Tom Kirlin's talent as a poet, his longstanding friendship to William Meredith, and the role he plays in continuing William's legacy. We should all be blessed with such friendship in life. This publication is a way to say thank you, to you and Katherine both over the years, and into the future.

As has been a kind of trademark for Poets' Choice, ENABLING LOVE includes a number of paintings by world-renowned artist Stoimen Stoilov (Stoimen-Stoilov.com). Soilov, like Kirlin has been a friend of Meredith and the foundation for many years, always willing to provide his extraordinary art for publication projects and whatever Bulgarian courtesies that may seem fitting. We are honored to have his exquisite work augment the winning manuscript.

I
You Move Among Us

"A poet penetrates a dark disguise
After his own conception, little or large.
Crossing the scaleless asia of trouble
Where it seems no one could give himself away,
He gives himself away, he sets a scale."

A Korean Woman Seated By A Wall

                    March

    or April

                there
                will be

            FROST

    p a r a d e s   complaints

                a

                    f
                        l   a
                    o
                            t

    of

            buck-
                naked   [poetic]

                        dreams

    HOWLing up
                Kitemaug
                    Road

        as
            a

                            Ch i l l

        brick   WiND

                cuts   its
                    sharp   teeth

on the
TANgled

      INNARDS

  of "We the   People"

for OH!   You

    & Far
                too

Many

                  Poets

LONGsince
             lie
    buried
in
  P
  a
  r
  a
  d
  i
  s
  e
      (Wyoming).

Yes you,   Sir William,   you & your

    Astringent
           Sweetwater

    WORDs

                     still wet
                           my
                                 whistle

                 &   warm
                       our
                                 Cheeks
Your poems
             as
                                 Fierce
as
                                 any
                                 Fleet
                                 of
                                 20ᵗʰ Century
                                 Poems

for
                       You
                             set
                                       Ablaze
                             the
                                       brute Heart

                       and Named
                                 (our divine)
                                           needs.

           Indeed:::
                             Your
                                       Flight

                                 deep
                                           inside

                                 the Psyche

EXPLODES

inside a Reader,

    FORcing

    U.S.
                to   EXamine

each Day
                    (more)
   Honestly, Freely

  (& for)
       whatever reason

WHATEVER
        we   wish
        to   become

        it   will
        not   be
          easy.

HOVERing

  now (slightly) beside

    VIGIL
    -ilant

    ENDuring
             words
    you keep

         (somewhat)

                                l o o
                   a   f

     Your   AIR   borne   Legacy
                                re ceding

                          though not completely

              for who can forget
                                        you

              Received

                          the PULITZER Prize

     Are recognized   by

                   The Academy of American Poets

              The Poetry Foundation

                          &
     The ENTIRE
                          nation

                   of Bulgaria

                   PLUS were
                        a Visiting Artist to
     Russia, India, Bulgria, Ireland, Greece.

                                        Yet
              the Norton Anthology

     dropped you (recently)
                          You,

                   a Cultured Voice,

               not even mentioned
               in the State Department's own

"American Poetry, 1945-1990: The Anti-Tradition."

                              True:

You are no
Anti-Traditonalist!

       You   strafed
                  us
                              with

       Sonnets   Villanelles

       Sestinas, etc.

                  (plus)

that   Constant RAPID

          Friendly

                              fire
          of
                     P
                     O
                     R
                     C
                     U
                     P
                     I
                     N
                     E
                                       rhymes

hitting each mark
                in the wee dark hours

of our wine-soaked
                MORTALity.

That   you do/did
        so
(well; repeatedly)
        stands as

    TESTament
          to
              Your
  own
          DIFFicult
            CHOices

                as you seized & accept
CONsequenCES
          disPLAYed

Compassion (wit)   COurage   duty

            Especially!
       in

    PARTIAL ACCOUNTS

(an Old Soul's war stories, told by its boyish KEEPer).

Yes, Sweet William, we COMMend and Thank You
          for
    (bringing into)   Being
a   more   Literate
    IMAGin ation.
  Now it is ours
      to Keep.

II
The Literate Imagination

"The ocean was salt before we crawled to tears."
The Wreck Of The Thresher

Your craft　　　seldom
　　　　　　　levitates/radiates

　　　　　BEAUTY.

　　　　　No. Your Carrier ship/words
　　　dredge deeper, lifting

　　　　　　　　　　b
　　　　　　　u　　　　　　m
　　S　　　　　　　　　　　　　e
　　　　　　　　　　　　　　　rged

　　　Grief
(oh, how you yearn for
　　　　　　　　　land
　　　　for Trees!)

　　　　mixing the body's　　Wet　Dirt

　　　　　with chaste hard Music

　　　　　so what I hear
　　　　　　　　　is
　Anglo-Saxon
　　　　　words

　　　　　that you hang　　　like　a

　　　　　WREATH
　　　　　　　　　　　of
　　dry-eyed　Love

　　　　　　　　around
　　　　　　　　　　　　　　OUR
　　(stiff) Necks,

　　　　　　　and so encourage US

to follow your

                        Warrior   spirit

     into the ENDLESS

           Battle That is Poetry
(which turns stone)
                          into
   flesh & being:

"Like that Greek boy whose name I now forget
Whose youth was one long study to cut stone;
One day his mallet slipped...
So that the marble opened on a girl
Seated at music and wonderfully fleshed
And sinewed under linen, riffling a harp;
At which he knew not that delight alone
The impatient muse intended, but, coupled with it, grief—
The harp-strings in particular were so light—
And put his chisel down for marveling on that stone."
                            A View of the Brooklyn Bridge

You chiseled
               Away

     at your   Soul

                 in so many ways,
knowing:

       "Poems are hard to read
       Pictures are hard to see
       Music is hard to hear
       And people are hard to love"
                    A Major [autobiographical] *Work*

And well before

your Craft

was half-grown, you poked about

                        life's

TRASHcans

          for bits of

half-NIBBLED

              Humanity

—and when caught
      like a Racoon

in the act, stood on your own two hind legs
and didn't back off.

Your
      (animal)
                  Instinct

for Survival
      your Intellect
   Command
   ing
        our singular
            Attention!!

     (precisely)
                    BEcause

You   so unflinchingly   examine

     the dog in every
     Man.

You stare at us
   looking

Up &

    D
    o
    w
    n

                                fearlessly

polishing the Form
                  in your Heart
                  our eyes, the souls

      and   INVITE
            us   In
                          demanding

we too   stAND

    Straight

    Keep time

        and MEASure

as   Together   we

    Navigate
        the unmoored

    Past   Present
            &   Future.

And, EVER the Raccoon,
          You

    Slow-Dance

    with   words

                    Athletically
                                with Wit & Heart-felt
Compassion
                                        as   if

                    HOPing to
                                        trap

the (half-
absent)
                                        Conscience.

                            Yes, as Muse, You

                                                rap at our door
                            Once Again,
                                        NEVER more

                                                tellingly
                                                than this,

                            the 10th year of your PASSing
                                    the 30th ANNIVERSARY

of
            Partial Accounts.

                                        Let us, therefore,
            Kind Reader,
                                        CELEbrate:

"The Muse and Her Gentleman"

I.

Touched by illiterate longing, he was like the man
Who could lay a hand across her heart
And you might think this is because his hand
Was unfamiliar, but, truth is, she
Had never had a man who was a friend.

Now he is both afraid of what she is
And does, and interested because she says she is
A dancer at a downtown gentlemen's club.

She could touch his arm, intimately,
Or not; he could send flowers, or flowery words,
To her hotel room, saying he is coming, or not.
He thinks he talks too much, and is not beloved.

What do you call this awkward silence which stands
Now between dead poets, honest praise & us—
We the living, naked, afraid; they, humble revenants?
Aren't time & death sufficient
To meet the requirement of love?

II.

True rememberance is neither rich, nor poor
Nor orphaned, nor vain, nor ignorant. Death is well-read;
Remberance pensive, private, unsettled, awake, irreverent
Deep inside us. In death, true friendship
Becomes neither sleep nor sufficient.

Once among the living, William is become a Muse
—Your daughter, my son, a love among us for words
Borne well after high school graduation.

This morning, on-line, feeling orphaned, she looks
For empty space. His grave is full. My page
Undone. A wicked wink and her will is one.
We write for less literate daughters and sons.

Still, she's touched. A tear runs, perhaps in raccoon
Sorrow. She looks hard at you—he at us
And laughs off these slight bumps, but not first before
Turning and sticking us with that wry, untimely smile.

You, Sir William the Pen, will never be
"A fresh joint/ tossed into damp sand."

III
It was May

"It was May
When things tend to look allegorical."
Roots

How
           did
                  you

      TRANSform
               yourself
     from
Ariel
        Warrior
                       to

          (grounded)
                    Poet?

Clearly, you joined a Company:

      Frost
Auden
Yeats
Lewis Thomas
Robert Penn Warren
      Other Poets

                      who
      dined (daily) on
                    NOTHING

                  but
               Harsh Truth
    Laughter
                    and
     (hard)
         Consequences.

      "Every last creature
      Is the one it meant to be."
          Consequences: ii. of love

                        HAUNTING
                        lines

                        that you applied
                                        to yourself
as well as
                        US
                                (admittiing)

                        you stole
                                into FROST's company

                                        with
                                        Lies

        (which) sometimes
                                        are necessary
                to gain
                                Admittance... no, rather
you sought

                                "respite from that blinding attention, [and]
                                More likely, a friendship
                                I felt I could only get by stealing."
                                                In Memory of Robert Frost

                                Another
                                        of your poetic
    Revelations
            is equally REVEALing:

                "Whatever death is, it sets pretenders free."
                                                For His Father

                                which then is
Exceeded
                                by these lines:

> "I have been, except on one occasion
> Myself. It is no good trying to be what you are not.
>
> We live among gangs who seem to have no stake
> In what we're trying to do, no sense of property or race,
> Yet if you speak with authority they will halt and break
> And suddenly, one by one, show you a local face."
>
> Consequences: iii my acts

Perhaps the
        Korean
              woman
made you do & say it,
                          the one
        who wore a mask
        of such Suffering

that you,
    William the Aviator,

              U
       A   L
V   T

        from your bomber's Seat

into Poetry & Teaching
        (LEAVing
        the AFFAIRS of War

                      to

                              the Grim Reaper).

And while you SPARE us
        the Grimace
                of war,
                        of say,
  Guernica,

        no doubt
                somedays
     you leaned
          FORward
                    behind your desk

     & wondered why
                the Young

          seem so easily

Distracted

     AD miring

                the color of their socks
                & the size of their
     Thighs,
  many for-   EVER

        Ignorant
      that soldiers
      lost more than
                    their

     METriCAL
     feet.

So yes, I Take Heart

     from your early Poetry, especially

>   your landing
>   of this Colliquy
>   with   your own
>
>   budding Muse,
>
>   Mrs. Leamington.

"Mrs. Leamington stood on a cloud
Quarreling with a dragon—it was May,
When things tend to look allegorical—
As I drove up the hill that silhouettes
Her house against the east. In any month
She's hard to place—scattered and sibylline:
She hangs the curtains for me in the fall
(Rather than let me ruin them myself)
And warns me about thieves and moths and women—
Nothing for money, all for neighborhood."

(Mrs. L, a fussy busybody, spies the root of Ambiguity's tree)

>   "And we rode the hairy serpent through the grass
>   To the edge of the rectangle she was turning up,
>   But he was saying nothing, by his depth
>   or diameter, about which way he'd come from."

Poet & Muse   you two pause
              for coffee.

That's when you, William the Pen
notice the root of all poetry
                        is (quite)
Quotidian:

>   "Dishtowels and her nylon underwear
>   Were on the clothes tree; straining at the door
>   Was her Mercedes. It was half past eight.
>   We sat in the kitchen on her good antiques.

'Have you ever really thought about the roots.'
She asked, filling a pair of luster cups,
'What a world they are, swaying in the thick air
Under us, upside down?'

Your answer would move Socrates:

                         I'd thought about them
All the week before, when the elms were budding...
And I'd thought how their roots all year around
Would keep that primavera delicacy.
So I said, 'I have, a little. What about them?'

That's when She(lley) says:

"'When I was a girl, my father put those cedars
In the hedge along the road. He told me then...
That a tree repeats its structure, up and down,
The roots mirroring the branches....'"

    (A mild disagreement ensues   about trees   in Fragonard)

     and Mrs. L (being Frostian)

   claims Shelley's   Figures
       look like... Roots.

No, more
     like coral, you, William the Aviator say.

        Mrs. Leamington (immediately) proceeds
to pull out her:

                 "book of reproductions
And showed me the lady swinging on the swing
In a mass of greenery and silk and cloud.
Then suddenly she turned it upside down
And the cloudy leaves and the clouds turned into rocks

And the boles of the tree were gripping them like rocks."

That's when Mrs. L. concludes her
        (poetic) Homily
                about Shelley, a Poet who
(as you so often do)

    "'...met his own image walking in the garden.
    That apparition, sole of men, he saw.
    For know there are two worlds of life and death:
    One which thou beholdest; but the other
    Is underneath the grave, where do inhabit
    The shadows of all forms that think and live,
    Till death unite them and they part no more....

    "'The strangest thing would be to meet yourself.
    Above the ground or below I wouldn't like it.'"
                                 Roots

Dear William, how far you have traveled
                from

    "War's unfeatured face"
                (where)

    "The far-off dying are her near affair;
    With her sprung creatures become weak or strong
She watches them down the sky and disappear,
    Heart gone, sea-bound, committed all to air."
                           Carrier

    William   Morris   Meredith, Jr.

I do believe
        your first TRULY
        stepped
              ashore

  from War's
      scalloped
blood-stained
        Seas
by walking

  through
    Shelly's MAZE

of Allegory.
      For, as you say:

"Shelley's houses and walks were always a clutter of women,
And god knows what further arrangements he kept in his mind.
Drole de menage, Rimbaud said of himself and Verlaine,
As if there were any other kind.
In Yeats' tower, in all that fakery of ghosts,
Some solid women came and slept as Mrs. Yeats' guests.
We are most our own strange selves when we are hosts."

          Five Accounts Of A
         Monagomous Man
         v. lines from his guest-book

So... back (for the moment)
  to Mrs. Lemington.

    Once scattered as a cloud,
    your Muse

  grew eager to go:

"'back to my spuds, she said. Don't you hate that word?
Yet it's good Middle English. Stop on your way home.
By then perhaps we'll both have earned a drink.'"
          Roots

William the Aviator has met his match, his Muse

                and Knows she

"...likes to split an apple down the middle
And with her hands behind her back ask them, which?
The other children fall in with the riddle
But he says, both hands! both hands, you sly old bitch!"

                              the poet as troublemaker"

Ah! Such a
      World-
      view

                brings

                with it

                A World
(of troubles).

A world
You
                take Root

      (and we)

grow into.

IV
The End of Deception

"There is no end to the
Deception of quiet things
And of quiet, everyday
People a lifetime brings."

The Chinese Banyan

>   The Korean War
>   exhumed
>   the
>   Grief
>   you carried
>   (always...)
>
> nay
>   Embraced
>   its Stoic musings
>
>   as you watched
>
>   Worlds at War
>   and
>   y/our
>   (Grecian)
>
>   Urn
>   shatter:

"...what is it in suffering dismays us more:
The capriciousness with which it is dispensed
Or the unflinching way we see it borne?
...
Ah, now she looks at me. We are unmasked
And exchange what roles we guess at for an instant.
The questions Who comes next and Why not me
Rage at and founder my philosophy.
Guilt beyond my error and grace past her grief
Alter the coins I tender cowardly,
Shiver the porcelain fable to green shards."

A Korean Woman
Seated By A Wall

No longer
>	content with such sentiments
>	>	as those you told yourself

>	in pastoral youth, when

>	>	>	"Days like today we are the clouds' men
>	>	>	And what they do all day is our concern."
>	>	>	*The Impressment*

You grew into

>	>	A Field of VISION

>	>	>	W i d e n ing

>	your reach
>	>	as you began to speak

>	>	>	Directly
>	>	>	to
>	>	>	your
>	>	>	audience.

Sentences   grow

>	>	COMMUNAL

>	—more than a few
>	laced with
>	>	(in)temperate
>	>	regret
that even Grief
>	can become
>	>	>	>	a commodity:
>	"My desperate friends, I want to tell
>	Them, you take too delicate offense

At the stench of time and man's own smell.
It is only the smell of consequence."

Consequences: i. of choice

Now, when you speak

    to a (post-war)
    Audience

        I feel each distance   GROW

        (as, quietly, we fall to y/our knees)

        and loudly praise

    St. Consequence
        as if sanity could take shore-leave

from War's Cathedral:

        "Let saints and painters deal
        With the mystery of likeness. As for him
        It scares him wide awake and dead alone.
        A man of action dials the telephone."
                              Barcelona

As your friend Auden said: "poetry changes nothing."
    [maybe; except those who read & write it?]

Such extreme feelings,

    grow (once, briefly)

        into a

        Self-Effacing
        Mask

(an affliction not uncommon at the time
of Berryman and Lowell)

which you later name:

Hazard, the Painter.

But before
    we wander on ahead
        let me
            P
                  E
           E
           K

                        at what

several ART - poems
            say

    about the

            LIMIitations
                          of

               Human Speech,

You start with the Body's Splendor:

"With flanks as clean as bone they signal one another
On the far side of a trench of music—
Such breasts and hair, such bold genitals
Until you would think we were the caged ones....

Yet it is not only their perfection detains
Us in the paunchy dark, it is pity too.
That they must signal that way, like eloquent mutes?

Yes, and a longer affliction of splendor:
That it cannot reproduce its kind."
The Ballet

This submerged admission
    of human-kind's limited

                Linguistic
                AMPLITUDE
    hums
                beneath

       the surface of your   own
SUBdued
       artistic order, Sir William, which

you later acknowledge:

    "It's not the tunes, although as I get older
    Arias are what I hum and whistle.
    It's not the plots—they continue to bewilder
    In the tongue I speak and in several that I wrestle.

    An image of articulateness is what it is:
    Isn't this how we've always longed to talk?

    ...these measured cries [opposite] the clumsy things we say
    In the heart's duresses, on the heart's behalf."
About Opera

    I may make more of what you see and feel or say

than you intend,

        the end of
            Self-Deception

        risks our discovering

a deeper truth

                —the Death of Empathy—

which
      HOVers
            just ahead

    for us

    and (if in
        forgetfulness)
  you.

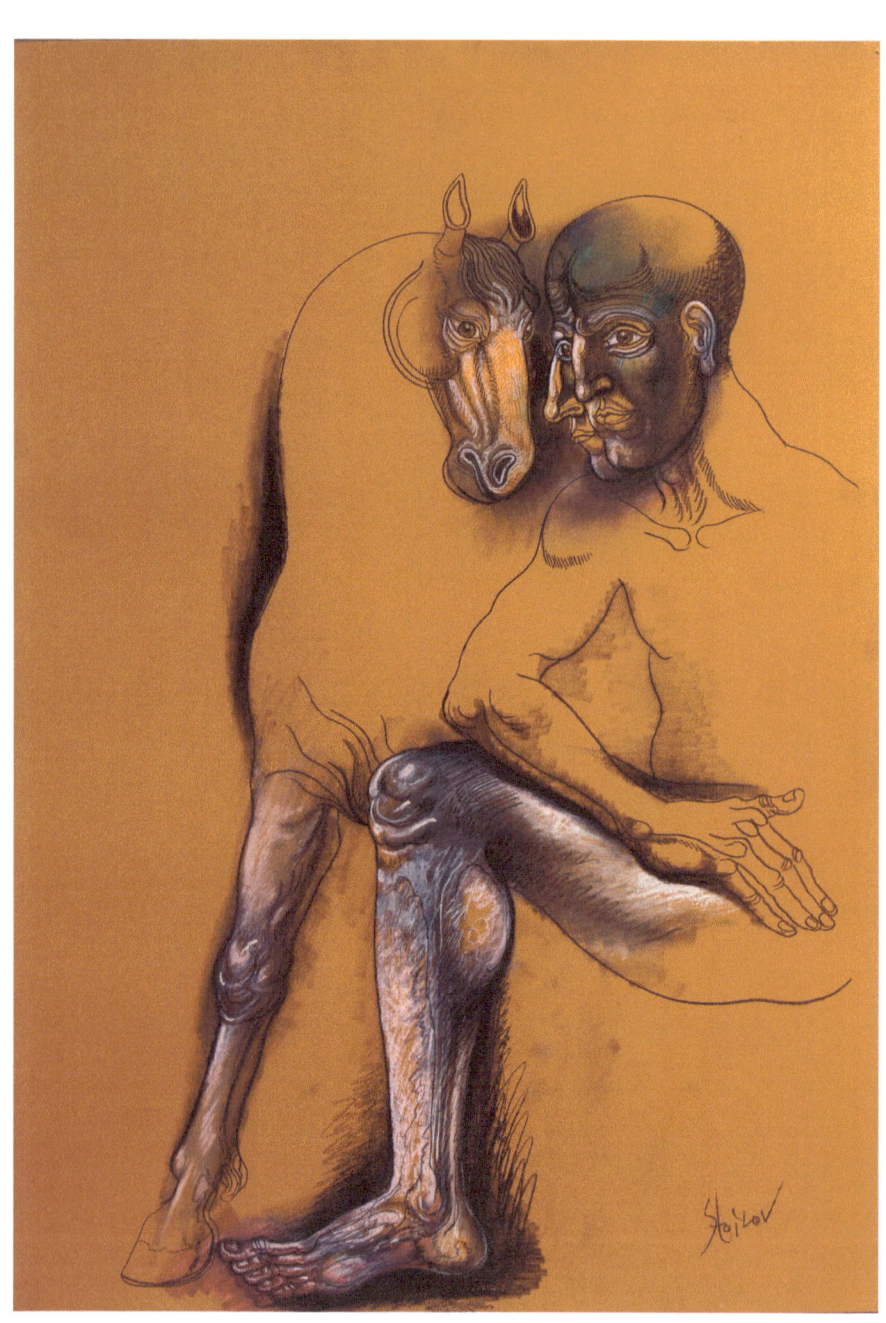

V
Self-Reckoning

"At the edge of the Greek world, I think, was a cliff
To which fallen gods are chained, immortal.
Time is without forgiveness, but intermittently
He sends the old, sentimental, hungry
Vulture compassion to gnaw on the stone
Vitals of each of us, even the young, as if
To ready each of us, even the old, for an unthinkable
Event he foresees for each of us—a reckoning, our own."
Last Things

Hazard the Painter

        is neither
        Greek god

nor
    shattered
        (Grecian) Urn.

        He is the MASK

    you   William the Artist

don
        (it seems to me)
        briefly

        to

        S P L   I   T

            yourself in two

  to   MOCK

      the world
    the limits of
   ART
        with wit
      and Irony.

    Life's PUNch
     line?

        The artist is

        "strickly a one-joke painter."

            [she/he must tell the truth]

Or, in Hazard's words, as he examines
Meredith's word-paintings:

"The fact that I don't like his pictures
should not obscure the facts
that he is a good man
that many admire his work (his canvases
threaten my existence and I hope
mine his, the intolerant bastard!)
that we are brothers in humanity
& the art. Often it does, though."

Hazard Faces a Sunday
in the Decline

Some might say this line of argument

CONFUSEs

    Biography
    mit
    Poetry

        but
        William
        launches

His self-critique

        by dangling

UP Side

        D
        O
        W
        N

            inside his

Craft
(literally).

"Harnessed and zipped on a bright
October day, having lied to his wife,
Hazard jumps, and the silk spanks
open, and he is falling safely.

This is what for two years now
he has been painting, in a child's palette
—not the plotted landscape that holds dim
below him, but the human figure dangling safe,
guyed to something silky, hanging here,
full of half-remembered instruction
but falling, and safe.

[Safe for now, but, like
                other poets
William carries
      an EXTRAordinary
              burden—what to make and say
              of the 1960s and 70s?]

He is in charge of morale in a morbid time.
He calls out to the sky, his voice
the voice of an animal that makes not words
but a happy incorrigible noise, not
of this time. The colors of autumn
are becoming audible though the haze.

It does not matter that the great masters
could see this without flight, while
dull Hazard must be taken up again and dropped.
He sees it. Then he sees himself....
Inside the bug-like goggles, his eyes water."
                                      Hazard's Optimism

This Icarus flight
—inward—to artistic
boundaries
         offers young poets
    rare
                 (and courageous)

          glimpses

of the
            IMAGINAtion

     in Limbo

        William
              talking to himself

           (wryly)

EXAMing

    his Life
        and Accomplishments

    his "Body of Work":

"I look out these two holes, or I run
into the other two and listen. Is Hazard trapped in here?

I have had on this funny suit for years, it's getting
baggy, but I can still move all the parts.....

People sometimes touch it, that feels good
although I am deep inside.

I do not find it absurd—is this because
I am used to it? (trapped in it? Where are we?
This is certainly not rubber or a cheap plastic.)

If I crawl out of it at night, it comes
snuffling after me and swallows me. It says

it is looking for pictures. I tell it
it has come to the wrong man."
                                                Where He's Staying Now

So what does the artist

                "in charge of morale in a morbid time"

see and say to himself?

            "Tonight Hazard's father and stepmother are having
            jazz for McGovern. In the old game-room
            the old liberals listen as the quintet builds
            crazy houses out of skin and brass, crumbling
            the house of decorum, everybody likes that.

            For decades they have paid for the refurbishing
            of America and they have not got their money's worth.
            Now they listen, hopeful,
            to the hard rock for McGovern."
                                                Politics

Long gone are the Allegories
the colloquies and
            DIALogue
                        with Shelly's Muse.

William the Walking Hazard

                                    a Revenant
            wandering through
                        Post-War society

                    steps
        past

                                        beer cans
                    & car accidents

and into a Lovely, yet Ancient
(forboding?) Landscape, where

                              "Ladyslippers,
                              gypsy plants long
                              absent, have come
                              back this cold May.
                              Erotic, stern
                              ambiguous
                              shapes, they can blight
                              or prosper a
                              season's footwork
                              for who finds them."

You, William (now turning back toward us)
      stop   to comtemplate

                              stones & Boulders
                                          (one)
                          as

LARGE
         as

       any Mastodon who

            "came riding here
      like hunters, on their ice-barges,
and where they debarked, they stay.

                    ***

Sometimes [Hazard] digs up sharpened ones,
flints- and quartzes-come-lately,
flown here on the ends of sticks
by hungier men, wrestled to earth
by rabbit or deer, little stones
who rode to their quiet on flesh-barges.

***

What is held in perpetuity? The town hall
with all the records will move off
one day, without legal notice.
The air that's passed through his lungs
or the love through his head and loins
are more his to keep than this boulder-camp,
ready to move off whenever the hunt resumes."
Squire Hazard Walks

    Lessons to be learned
        from
          Oblivion??

"He's with Yeats, for adult education—
hand-clapping lessons for the soul,
compulsory singing lessons for the soul,
in his case, tone-deaf.
He agrees with Auden, old people can show
'what grace of spirit can create,'
modeling the flesh when it's no longer flashy.
That's the kind of lift he wants to his jowls....

And there *is*
    a way Forward
(One which Mrs. Leamington would approve):

He is founding a sect for the radical old
freaks you may call them but you're wrong,
who persist in being at home in the world,
who just naturally feel it's a good bind to be in,
let the young feel as uncanny as they like.
Oldbodies, he calls them affectionately
as he towels his own in the morning
in front of the mirror, not getting any flashier.
He thinks about Titan and Renoir a lot
in this connection. Nothing is unseemly

that takes it rise in love. If only his energy lasts."
His Plans For Old Age

But getting here
has meant
expending so much
(poetic) energy

Repetition
has begun to set in:

"Here at the seashore they use the clouds over & over again, like rented animals in *Aida*."
Rhode Island

Quietly, as you lift Hazard's
Mask

you, William Meredith,

give us back

a

(FRACTured)

Poetic VOICE

in uncanny notes
that warmly
recall

Yeats, at Prayer

in search of
Belief:

"Enabling love, roof to this drafty hutch...
take care of the haunts who stay with us here.

In a little space for a long while they've walked
wakeful when we sleep, averting their sad glance
when we're clumsy with one another, they look
at something we can't look at yet, they creak the boards
beside the bed we creak, in some hard durance.

And if we're weary at night what must they be?
Bed them like us at last under your roof.

***

[W]ishing our sibling spirits nothing but good,
let them see these chambers once with the daylight eyes
you lend to lovers for our mortal time.
Or change some loveless stalker into me
before my bone-house clatters into lime."

The Ghosts of the House

And your

    E
    N
    ABLING   Love

is spoken to one person
and to ALL the living:

"What you have given me,
in these long moments when our words
come back, or breaths come back,
is a whole man at last,
and keeping me, remembers:

On deck one night, the moon past full
coming up over the planet's edge,
the big globe ripping its skin,
the smaller already accepting its waning

and talking about vast skiey distances.
I had not met you yet.
Aft, the aircraft folded like mantises,
ahead and abeam, destroyers running like hounds,
and the wind.

A sentry walked off
the rolled front of the flight deck,
crying *oh* as he fell to the sea.
Lost in the cold skin of the globe,
he cried *oh* for less than, panted
for less than love, going away,
the loneliest noise that ever wound in my ear.

February 14

No longer
    at Sea,

    you've firmly
    Planted
    your Feet

in American Literature,

        your Poems
    have become
      Sentries
        to every
          attentive
          Generation:

"Gnawed by a vision of rightness
that no one else seems to see,
what can a man do
but bear witness?

And what has he got to tell?
Only the shaped things he's seen—
a few things made by men,
a galaxy made well.

Though more of each day is dark,
though he's awkward at the job
he squeezes paint from the tube.
Hazard is back at work.
Winter: He Shapes Up

And yet....

        Bear
Witness

            to

                    what?

            And how long, how Large

      grows

                    DARKness????

VI
The Center Cannot Hold

"When I wake up, what am I to do
with this mortifying life I've saved again?"

Freezing. iv

The first hint is more than a hunch:

> "I dreamt once they caught me and, holding me down,
> Burned my genitals with gasoline;
> In my stupid terror I was telling them names
> So my manhood kept and the rest went up in flames.
>
> 'Now, say the world is a fair place,' the biggest one said,
> And because there was no face worse than my own there
> I said it and got up. Quite a lot of me is charred.
> By our code it is fair. We play fair. The world is fair."
> *Consequences. iii. my acts*

And still the question hangs there
      as if, like Hazard,

upside/down:

> "what am I to do
> with this mortifying life I've saved again?

You answer yourself with a parable:

> v.
>
> To live out our lives under a good tyrant
> is a lot to ask, the old man said.
> There are reports that the swaggering brothers
> and their wives and foreign in-laws
> are shouting again, in the marble house
> that looks down on the harbor and the town.
> We know what they are capable of,
> quarreling with one another
> and in contention with the gods.
> We keep indoors.
> Impatience and ignorance sometimes ignite
> in a flash of bravery among us,
> he said. It is usually inappropriate.

vi

> Some normal excellence, of long accomplishment
> is all that can justify our sly survivals.
> *Freezing*

Your answer, I believe, builds on an earlier dream:

> "(*Sea-brothers, I lower to you the ingenuity of dreams,*
> *Strange lungs and bells to excape in; let me stay aboard last—*
> We amend our dreams in half-sleep. Then it seems
> Easy to talk to the severe dead and explain the past.
> Now they are saying, *Do not be ashamed to stay alive,*
> *You have dreamt nothing that we do not forgive.*
> And gentlier, *Study something deeper than yourselves,*
> *As, how the heart, when it turns diver, delves and saves.)*"
> The Wreck of the Thresher

As does the artistic mask that
    first surfaced and

        "settled like a sly disguise
        On [the Korean woman's] cheerful old face."

In old age, there is nothing hiding
    to or for or from.

"Like black duennas the hours sit
And read our lips and watch our thighs.
The years are pederasts: they wait
for boys and will not meet my eyes.

Two shapes it has traced honor this right hand:
The curve that a plane rides out
As it leaves or takes a deck on the scalloped sea...

> And... his gauche fellow, moving symetrically
> Having described one body so well
> They could dress that shape in air...."
> *Five Accounts of the Monogomous Man*

Your Enabled Love

        slips an arm

             around

             Richard's

                        waist,

     He who meets your

Revenant

        in lost shapes

    He who carries

        Your   Weight

            up
            &   D
                 O
                   W
                     N

        stairs, tending

to the

        Legacy.

    All of which is as
it should be, for:

> "The light
> of love gilds but does not alter.
> People don't change one another....
>
> The only correction is
> by you of you, by me of me....
>
> every last creature
> is the one it meant to be."
> *Consequences: Of Love*

Kind words that open a door
 to Harsh Reality,

    dear William the Pen,

(especially)

IF? If?? When???

one Applies

that Wisdom
to your

Later Poetic career

which begins
with this sentiment:

VII
Efforts at Speech

"Cheer or courage is what [poems] were all born in.
It's what they're trying to tell us, miming like that.
It's native to the words,
and what they want us always to know,
even when it seems quite impossible to do."

The Cheer

Having
                  Praised, Honored,
                  nay, Believed

Shelley Auden Frost Yeats

        (so lawyerly the way

        EACH
        adjudicates
    fear/   speech)

you now measure
        yourself (harshly)
against

        COnTEmporaries
                        (generously,
            repeating each
            given name
            a telling feat)

        Richard Wilbur
    Wallace Stevens
        Robert Lowell (again)
        Ernest Hemingway
        Sylvia Plath
        John Berryman (again and again)
        Kurt Vonnegut
        Sigmund Freud
    Until a

        STROKE
                tore You r

```
                    T
                    O      from    B
                    N              R      from    L
            G              A                      I
                    U              I                      M
                    E              N                      B....
```

"Expressive Aphasia"

                                                  doctors

   call it.

        But   it seems

(to me)   you

                            already

KNEW   and had NAMED
                        it:

"*Effort at Speech.*"

                    And   (again)

It's a

                brown-faced

    boy
            of fifteen or sixteen
                  (his face "phrased
                  like a question")

        who ROBS
              you of the Pen:

"Half of the papers lending me a name are
                  gone with him nameless"

Your Wreck

                                 (still)

    produces

    Anguish

                        Hope Suffering

                                     among dear Friends

but most
(in retrospect)

                I suspect

Calm

    in those who never

Claimed

    your embrace

                or shared

    your keen
    ATTention.

So, later, after

    Adult On-set Autism,

                        to

watch   you swim
                the
                Ocean of

    COURAGE
        makes us all want to

C
    R A
        W
            L

through tears.

        Even as You

            Lamented

                SUIcide

      among writers, Poets, Friends

(and yet)
    REFUSed
                to
                sink

                        into
                        Depression

        or   self-pity.

Instead, on first meeting you
I Imagined
            Your
                  Imagination

(looking out those holes)

Not as Hazard, behind a mask

        but an an ARTist robbed of

                Expressive
                Anticipation,
                who kept:

"Walking home [as] I fraternized with
shadows, Zig-zagging with them where they flee the streetlights,
Asking for trouble, asking for the message
                                      trouble had sent me.

All fall down has been scribbled on the street in
Garbage and excrement: so much for the vision
Others taunt me with, my untimely humor,
                                      so much for cheerfulness.

Next time don't wrangle, give the boy the money,
Call across chasms what the world you know is.
Luckless and lied to, how can a child master
                                      human decorum?

Next time a switch-blade, somewhere he is thinking,
I should have killed him and took the lousy wallet.
Reading my cards he feels a surge of anger
                                      blind as my shame.

Error from Babel mutters in the places,
Cities apart, where now we word our failures:
Hatred and guilt have left us without language
                                    who might have held discourse.
                                              Effort at Speech

        No longer submerged
Grief
                stakes
      its
                        (starker)
                        claim
                        to
                        Days of Silent Sanity:

"Whether we give assent to this or rage
Is a question of temperament and does not matter.
Some will has been done past our understanding,
Past our guilt surely equal to our fears.
Dullards, we are set again to the cryptic blank page
Where the sea schools us with terrible water.
The noise of a boat breaking up and its men is in our ears.
The bottom here is too far down for our sounding.
The ocean was salt before we crawled to tears.
                    The Wreck of the Thresher

Silence

      alone

                    answers that "sly old bitch"
                    of youth

         who hides Poetic Truth

                          (from all of us)

     and holds out

              Both Hands
              like:

"The woman who sailed her dinghy out in the Bay
in the fall blow—autumn is for beginnings—
and was found miles from the zig-zagging sailboat
that she knew like a husband—either she sought
a way to drown or the Chesapeake taught her, not both.

Either before I die I'll falter and tell
the strange secret I was given once as a token
or I'll manage to carry it with me.

Somebody knows or nobody knows these answers.

One of those appalling things is true too."
                                       Not Both

                    Equally true

William, is your Strength
         of Spirit

which shines
                    through

          a second "Crossing Over"

                    (into)

poetic SPEECH:

          "That's what love is like. The whole river
          is melting. We skim along in great peril,

          having to move faster than ice goes under
          and still find foothold in the soft floe."
                              Crossing Over

And, though said to one, you shared with us all in poetry:

          "How perilous in one another's V
          our lives are, yoked in this yoke:
          two men, leaning apart for light,
          but in a wind who give each other lee."
                              A Couple of Trees

VI
Impartial Laugher

"It is like finding on your tongue
right words to call across the floe
of arrogance to the wise dead,
of health to sickness, old to young
Across this debt, we tell you so."

Talking Back
[To W. H. Auden]

              What
                  (more)
                            do
                we LIVing
                              owe

                    you

                    who
                    M
                          o
                          v
                                  e

    (among)   US

                  like a chill breeze

                                    Scattering

    Memorials, Birthdays, holidays, Poems, Trips,

              Lovers, Articles, Books

    Prizes
                              &
                                            such

                        Generosity

          that   ARTeries of
                          Friendship

              harden into trees

                      that a Racoon

      would love to climb
                even for the   Briefest

chance to meet???

Beyond reading
your Essays, Reviews
Meeing   the Acolytes   Students

Revisting Conversations
       Praising the Grants, Awards

(twice, you were honored by the Library of Congress)

       We take
       Pleasure

in your Feast
of   Poems

              gristled
                      with   Hard Truths.

And,   Yes,   of course,

       we still will visit
       you in

       (new)

       LONDON
                      Connecticut
                              (your ashes also
       in
               Bulgaria's
Rila Monestary).

       But mostly
              (and most personally)

                      I will continue to

REcall

                    that first meeting
         at your party, in Bethesda, Maryland.

         I had not yet greeted you
         properly
                   (even on a poetic
                    trip)
but in that private session
you asked me to recite a poem
and once I did, you gripped affliction
by the throat and troubled out
fair words and lasting impressions.

         Afterwards, happy to be included
         you moved among we chatty few
         picking up lipsticked glasses
         from coffee tables, placing some
         on countertops

         as through it all, smiled and nodded encouragement
         at this or that thought, a turn of phrase, caught
         expressions. You clearly lived, in silence
         the spellbound muse, then of a tender age
         somewhat of scattered tongue
         full of goodwill, grace and emotions unsung.

         I suppose we relish most what most we choose
         but like that witch who demanded
         in youth one hand, you answered "both"
         and now, in age, your smile
         wryly countered: "neither."

         We poets often break one simple rule,
          the truce between silence, death and
         truth —and so sing out childish unfit
         rhymes until in time life masters us
         and we become finger-food.

Meantime, patterned as china, you gathered us
up that day, filling the room with senseless music.
Your crooked smile outlasts
the body, your poems now our muse.

VI
Epilogue

Why the Soul Loves Catfish
             To William Meredith

Let's just say an elegant man
in a loose blue nightcap
with nothing, nothing on his mind
but the sky, surprised us
tracking game by starlight

shot you in the blind
made off with the lamps
of madness & climbed
scattering as ransom
this palpable absence

only time can refine—
swirling her honey head
making our bed, as constant
as taxes & crime....So welcome
if you can, ladies & gentlemen

an old roommate of mine:
a son of a gun—a hell
of a guy—a cat whose ass
rattles buckshot—the warden
my soul, serving life, plus 99.

Examples of Created Systems

    For Robert Penn Warren and Eleanor Clark

i. the stars

We look out at them on clear nights, thrilled
rather than comforted—brilliance and
distance put us in mind of our

own burnings and losses. And then who
flung them there, in a sowing motion
suggesting that random is beautiful?

ii. archipelagoes

Or again, the islands that the old
cartographers, triangulating
their first glimpses of bays and peaks, set
down, and which the rich traveler, from
a high winter chair, chooses among
today—chains of jade thrown across the
torso of the sea-mother, herself
casually composed.

iii. work camps and prisons

The homeless
Solzhenitsyn, looking at Russia,
saw a configuration of camps
spotting his homeland, 'ports' where men
and women were forced to act out
the birth-throes of volcanic islands,
the coral patience of reefs, before
a 'ship,' a prison train, bore them down
that terrible archipelago
conceived and made by men like ourselves.

iv. those we love

Incorrigibly (it is our nature)
when we look at a map we look for
the towns and valleys and waterways
where loved people constellate, some of
them from our blood, some from our own loins.
This fair scattering of matter is
all we will know of creation, at
first hand. We flung it there, in a learned
gesture of sowing—random, lovely.

–William Meredith

ARTIST'S BIOGRAPHY

Stoimen Stoilov

1944　Born in Varna (Bulgaria)
1972　Graduated from the Academy of Fine Arts in Sofia (Bulgaria).
Lives and works in Vienna (Austria) since 1991.

ONE-PERSON EXHIBITIONS IN:

Australia, Austria, Bulgaria, Canada, Czech Republic, France, Finland, Germany, Italy, Japan, Luxembourg, Norway, Russian Federation, Slovakia, Sweden, Switzerland, United States of America.

BIENNALES AND SALONS

Print Biennale, Varna (Bulgaria); Europ Art, Geneva (Switzerland); International Print Triennale, Chamallières (France); Biennale des artistes jurassiens, Delemont (Switzerland); Print Biennale, Ljubljana (Slovenia); Salon d'automne, Paris (France); Print Biennale, Fredrikstad (Norway); Print Biennale, Cracow (Poland); International Print Exhibition, Biella (Italy); Art Expo, New York (USA); Salon du dessin et de la peinture à l'eau, Paris (France); Print Biennale, Sao Paulo (Brazil); Biennale, Brno (Czech Republic); Biennale, Bratislava (Slovakia)

PRIZES

2009　The title Professor
1991　Gottfried von Herder Prize for his complete works, University of Vienna (Austria)
1991　Prize at the 2nd Print Triennale, Chamallières (France)

1985   Grand Prix for Bulgarian Participants at the 3rd Print Biennale, Varna (Bulgaria)
1984   Prize at Art Expo, New York (USA), granted by the foundation Bilan de l'art contemporain.
1983   The 'Iliya Petrov' Grand Prix for Mural Painting awarded by the Union of Bulgarian Artists, Sofia (Bulgaria)
1982   Silver Medal at the International Exhibition in Leipzig (Germany)
1976   Grand Prix of the Biennale, Brno (Czech Republic)

He has been awarded many other national prizes for print and drawing.

PRIVATE COLLECTIONS AND MUSEUMS

Austria
Museum of Graphic Art Albertina, Vienna
Vienna Ministry of Foreign Affairs, Vienna
Artothek, Vienna

Bulgaria
The National Art Gallery, Sofia
Municipal Museum of Art, Varna

France
Bibliothque nationale de France, Paris
Fonds national d'art contemporain, Paris
Art Dialogue Foundation, Paris

Germany
Museum of Art Villa Merkel, Esslingen
Museum of Graphic Art of the Schreiner Foundation, Bad Steben
Ludwig Forum, Aachen

Russia
Pushkin Museum of Art, Moscow

USA.
The Library of Congress, Washington DC
New York Public Library
Princeton University
Yale University
Florida State University (Strozier Library)
Florida Atlantic University (Jaffe Collection)
Middlebury College (Starr Library)

Works in private collections:
Austria, Australia, Bulgaria, France, Finland, Germany, Japan, Luxembourg, Norway, Sweden, and the United States of America.

AUTHOR'S BIOGRAPHY

Tom Kirlin won the Larry Neal Award for Poetry. He also received a grant from the District of Columbia Commission on the Arts and a fellowship from the National Endowment for the Humanities for post-doctoral studies at Yale University.

Kirlin taught at the University of Wisconsin-Madison before moving to Washington, D.C. Here, he worked for several decades on energy, environment, science and technology policy issues, including the UN climate negotiations that led to the Kyoto Protocols. He later served as Vice President of the Center for the Study of the Presidency, a non-partisan group he helped rebuild as a staff and Board member.

Following a summer at Bread Loaf, the Little Red Tree Press published his first book of poems, *Under the Potato Moon,* in 2013. Other poems have appeared in *Hungry as We Are, The WPFW Poetry Anthology,* and *Cabin Fever.* His wife, Katherine, and he helped celebrate the Smithsonian Institution's 25th Folklife Festival by collecting and authoring the *Smithsonian Folklife Cookbook.*

[Photo by Kate Kirlin]

www.ingramcontent.com/pod-product-compliance
Lightning Source LLC
Chambersburg PA
CBHW041219070526
44584CB00001B/16